CAMEROON TRAVEL GUIDE 2024:

Discovering Cameroon's beauty and treasures, including top restaurants and accommodations

Havilah F. Mills

All rights reserved. No part of this publication may be reproduced, distributed, or transmitted in any form or by any means, including photocopying, recording, or other electronic or mechanical methods, without the prior written permission of the publisher, except in the case of brief quotations embodied in critical reviews and certain other noncommercial uses permitted by copyright law.

Copyright © 2024 Havilah F. Mills

Table of Contents

Introduction to Cameroon
Organizing your trip to Cameroon
Getting to and around Cameroon
Accommodation options in Cameroon
Exploring Yaoundé- the Capital City
Discovering Douala—the Economic Center
Natural Wonders in Cameroon
Cameroon Cultural Immersion
Outdoor Activities and Adventure
Historical and Cultural Sites
Savoring cuisine from Cameroon
Departure and Travel Tips

Chapter 1

Introduction to Cameroon

Overview of Cameroon

Located in Central Africa on the Gulf of Guinea, Cameroon is a nation distinguished by its intricate history, stunning natural surroundings, and rich cultural variety. With more than 250 different ethnic groups represented in its people, the country's diverse tapestry of languages, traditions, and customs is enhanced by this.

Geographically speaking, Cameroon has a diverse terrain that includes savannas, verdant rainforests, and the towering Mount Cameroon, Central Africa's highest point. Its fauna reflects this richness as well; the nation is home to a wide variety of animals, including gorillas, elephants, and many rare bird species.

After World War I, Germany colonized Cameroon, which was then split between France and Britain. Cameroon attained independence in 1960. The political, social, and economic environment of the country has been profoundly shaped by this historical context. Bilingualism is encouraged by the official languages of France and English, which both represent the colonial past.

Natural resources such as oil, wood, and agricultural items are Cameroon's economic assets. However, the country has problems with inequality between urban and rural regions, corruption, and inadequate infrastructure. The government is working to solve these problems and encourage sustainable growth.

The vibrant culture of Cameroon is reflected in its traditional music, dances, and festivals. The nation is proud of its football skills, and both domestic and international events are enthusiastically supported. The political capital of Yaoundé and the commercial center of Douala function as the centers of government and trade, while several areas add unique characteristics to the national character.

In summary, Cameroon is a country dedicated to tackling issues for a more affluent future, with a rich past and a broad range of cultures. Its voyage demonstrates the tenacity of a people negotiating the confluence of modernity and tradition in the center of Africa.

Variations in Culture

Known as "Africa in Miniature," Cameroon is a cultural kaleidoscope that has an astounding range of races, languages, and customs. The nation, home to over 250 unique ethnic groups, is a prime example of amicable cross-cultural cohabitation, fostering a lively and dynamic social fabric.

Cameroon has an impressive linguistic variety, with more than 200 distinct languages spoken across the country. Because of the nation's colonial past, the Anglophone and Francophone areas make up the majority of this linguistic patchwork. Even though French and English are the official languages, several regional tongues—including Duala, Fulfulde, and Bamileke—remain alive and well, maintaining distinctive cultural subtleties.

In Cameroon, every ethnic group contributes its own traditions, rituals, and creative manifestations. Storytelling, dance, and traditional music are essential for maintaining and transferring cultural legacies. The rhythms of Cameroon's varied musical environment are complemented by the rhythms of the Sahelian North, the Bikutsi in the south, and the Makossa in the center.

Different ethnic groups' traditional clothing serves as a visual display as well as a symbolic representation of their identity and history. A feeling of pride and belonging is conveyed via intricate beading, vibrant textiles, and unique designs, which highlight the rich cultural tapestry weaved across the country.

Cameroon's diversified culinary landscape is a reflection of the abundance of high-quality local resources available. The culinary variety of the nation reflects its many ecosystems, ranging from the spicy foods of the Sahel area to the plantain and cassava-based cuisine in the Central and Southern regions.

Festivals and cultural events highlight Cameroon's vast variety even more. A few vivid occasions that demonstrate the country's rich cultural diversity include the Nguon Festival in

Bamenda, the Ngondo Festival in Douala, and the colorful festivals of the Fulani people.

The promotion of cultural appreciation and understanding is still being worked on, despite the difficulties that some language and ethnic groups confront. In order to promote unity among varieties, organizations and projects aim to preserve and promote indigenous languages, traditional arts, and traditions.

Essentially, Cameroon's cultural variety is a living, breathing monument to the people's tenacity and inventiveness, rather than just a statistical figure. It is an ongoing celebration of cultures, languages, and traditions that come together to make up this extraordinary African country's distinct character.

Climate and geography

Situated on Africa's west-central coast, the landscape of Cameroon is as varied as its cultural fabric. Cameroon's strategic position has shaped its history and development.

The tremendous geographical variance of Cameroon's terrain is its most notable attribute. The terrain is a patchwork of habitats, ranging from the savannas of the north to the thick rainforests in the south. Dominating the southwest is the majestic Mount Cameroon, the tallest mountain in Central Africa and an active volcano that contributes to the nation's climatic variability in addition to providing amazing vistas.

The Gulf of Guinea's coastal lowlands give way to a lush belt of rainforests that is home to a wide variety of wildlife. This area is distinguished by a network of rivers, including the Sanaga and Nyong, lush forest, and significant rainfall. The country's geological dynamism is shown by the towering plateaus and volcanic vistas that appear as one travels inside.

Large savannas and semi-arid conditions define the increasingly dry and Sahelian environment found in the north. This area is traversed by the Benue River and its tributaries, which sustain agriculture and act as a vital community lifeblood.

There are two distinct rainy seasons in Cameroon, usually spanning from March to June and September to November; however, the severity of each season varies by location. While the northern parts are distinguished by a more prominent dry season, the southern section of the nation gets more rainfall, which adds to the lushness of the rainforest.

Cameroon's climate is significantly influenced by its varied landscape. The interior has a tropical climate, whereas coastal regions have a humid equatorial environment. The Saharan air masses have an impact on the northern areas, which are often hotter and drier.

The diverse topography and climate of Cameroon affect the country's flora and fauna as well as the way of life of its people. A vital economic sector, agriculture is reliant on the various climates and produces a wide range of crops, from millet and sorghum in the north to cocoa and oil palms in the south.

Essentially, Cameroon's climate and geography combine to form an enthralling mosaic that molds the country's natural beauty and residents' way of life, making it a nation with a complex landscape just waiting to be discovered and comprehended.

Please be aware that the placement of the images in this book may not be properly aligned, but it's to give you a glimpse of what you may likely see in Cameroon.

Chapter 2

Organizing your trip to Cameroon

Ideal Time to Go

Your choices and the experiences you want to have will play a major role in determining the ideal time to visit Cameroon. The nation, which is in Central Africa, has a diversified geography, with hilly areas and coastal plains contributing to its changeable climate.

November through February is considered the perfect dry season for individuals who like the outdoors and animals. The temperature is somewhat cooler during this time of year, and animals like gorillas and elephants are more active. At this time of year, the well-known Dja Faunal Reserve, a UNESCO World Heritage Site, is especially enticing.

If you're more interested in cultural events, scheduling a trip around December's holiday season gives you the chance to see lively celebrations and customs. During this period, Cameroonians enjoy a variety of cultural activities that provide a unique window into the rich cultural legacy of the nation.

However, the best time to explore hilly areas like the Cameroon Highlands if you're an adventure seeker and like trekking is during the dry season. The beautiful scenery is a delight for those who like the outdoors, and the weather is ideal for outdoor activities.

It's important to remember that there are geographical differences, with the southern coastal regions experiencing a more tropical climate with greater annual rainfall. No matter what time of year you visit these places, you should be ready for sporadic downpours of rain.

To sum up, the ideal time to go to Cameroon will depend on your interests and the particular area you want to see. A unique and pleasurable trip to this varied African country may be ensured by carefully considering the weather patterns and regional temperatures, regardless of your interests in animals, cultural experiences, or outdoor activities.

Entry and visa requirements

To ensure a seamless and pleasurable journey to Cameroon, visitors must understand the country's visa and admission regulations. A thorough awareness of the admission procedures is essential to making the most of your trip to Cameroon, which has a broad variety of landscapes, from lush rainforests to barren savannahs.

First of all, except for inhabitants of some African nations, travelers to Cameroon must get a visa prior to their arrival. You may apply for a business or tourist visa, depending on your country of citizenship. For the most recent details and application instructions, it is advised that you visit the official website of the Cameroonian embassy or consulate in your nation.

Travelers often need to provide a valid passport that is valid for at least six months beyond the planned departure date in addition to a visa. Upon admission, certain passengers could additionally be required to provide documentation of their yellow fever vaccine. This is a usual requirement since yellow fever is so common in the area.

The main airports for travelers arriving in Cameroon by air are either Yaoundé or Douala International Airports. Arriving by land, visitors may find entrance points at several border crossings. Understanding the unique entry point policies and processes is crucial.

Comprehending the local traditions and cultural norms is also essential for an easy transition into Cameroon. Courtesies and deference are much valued, and a kind salutation often suffices. Furthermore, observing local laws and ordinances is necessary for a trouble-free vacation.

It's also a good idea to keep up with any changes or travel warnings issued by your government. Political and social conditions might change; therefore, it will be helpful to you to organize your trip more efficiently if you are aware of any possible obstacles.

In conclusion, the most important things for visitors to Cameroon to remember are to make sure they have the required immunizations, follow local laws, and make sure their visa requirements are met. By doing this, you may provide yourself with access to a fulfilling experience in a nation that is known for its varied natural beauty and rich cultural tapestry.

Ideas for Itineraries for Travel

A Cameroonian travel schedule must balance the country's varied landscapes, rich cultural legacy, and distinctive attractions. Cameroon has a diverse range of activities that may be expertly combined to create an unforgettable trip, catering to the interests of adventure seekers, wildlife enthusiasts, and cultural vultures alike.

Start your journey in the capital city of Yaoundé, where you can fully experience the bustling metropolitan lifestyle. To learn more about the history and cultural development of Cameroon, visit the National Museum. The Basilica of Our Lady of Peace is a magnificent building that provides sweeping views of the city. Don't miss it.

Take off for the beach city of Douala from Yaoundé. Savor the regional food at the waterfront eateries and explore the vibrant markets, such as Marché des Fleurs. The vibrant environment and busy streets provide an insight into the ever-evolving metropolitan culture.

For those who love the outdoors, a trip to Limbe is essential. Limbe, tucked away at the foot of Mount Cameroon, provides the ideal fusion of beach and jungle pleasures. The black sand beaches provide a peaceful retreat, while the Limbe Wildlife Centre is a sanctuary for monkeys.

Visit Cameroon's western highlands for an excursion that is a little further off the beaten track. Discover the charming Bamenda Highlands, where quaint settlements and terraced slopes provide a tranquil haven. The Bafut Palace, which is close by, offers information about the area's cultural history.

The Ring Road's breathtaking scenery must be experienced in order for a trip to Cameroon to be considered complete. This loop route passes by picturesque Lake Awing, historic towns, and plenty of vegetation. Don't pass up the chance to see the magnificent Twin Lakes, a natural marvel encircled by lush hills.

The tallest mountain in Central and West Africa, Mount Cameroon, is a great place to hike for an exhilarating experience. Along with being a strenuous hike, the climb offers breathtaking views of the surrounding countryside.

Go into Cameroon's northern regions to finish your adventure. Discover the Sahelian scenery around Maroua, where the Fulani people's many wares are on display in traditional marketplaces. Elephants, giraffes, and other species may be seen in their natural environment in Waza National Park.

All things considered, a comprehensive travel plan for Cameroon includes the vibrant metropolitan landscapes, varied natural attractions, and cultural treasures that make this country in West Africa unique. Cameroon offers a trip that surpasses expectations, whether you're seeing animals, seeing busy towns, or hiking through jungles.

Chapter 3

Getting to and around Cameroon

Getting to Cameroon by flight

You must first choose your departure place if you want to fly to Cameroon. Begin by looking for flights from the closest international airport that are currently available. To make the most affordable and practical choices, use internet travel portals or speak with travel brokers.

Take into consideration well-known carriers like Air France, Brussels Airlines, or Turkish Airlines that provide flights from other countries to Cameroon. To choose a flight that best fits your needs, compare costs, travel times, and layover locations.

Make sure your passport is up-to-date and find out whether you need a visa to visit Cameroon based on your nationality. Make sure you have all the required vaccines, and check the most recent entrance requirements—these sometimes vary.

Plan your travel far in advance to take advantage of the lowest prices and departure times. Consider the length of layovers when selecting flights, and make sure they fit within your timetable. Don't forget to account for any possible COVID-19 procedures or travel limitations that could impact your trip.

Consider the weather and any specialized products you may need for your trip to Cameroon while packing. As your departure time and terminal get closer, double-check all the specifics of your flight.

On the day of your trip, go to the airport early to give yourself enough time for security checks, check-in, and any unforeseen delays. To guarantee a seamless boarding experience, abide by airport and airline regulations.

When you arrive in Cameroon, go through immigration and customs. Make sure you have your passport, visa, and any relevant health certificates on hand, along with any other essential documentation. To get to your location, familiarize yourself with the local transit choices.

To summarize, meticulous study, careful assessment of airline alternatives, adherence to entrance restrictions, and preparation for a smooth travel experience are all necessary when booking a journey to Cameroon.

International Airports

There are many international airports in Cameroon, which are important entry points to this richly diversified and geographically diverse country in Central Africa. Douala International Airport and Yaoundé Nsimalen International Airport are the two main international airports.

1. International airport in Douala:

Douala International Airport, located in Cameroon's commercial center, is a busy hub with state-of-the-art amenities. It provides a selection of international flights linking Cameroon with different locations throughout the globe. Passengers may travel in luxury thanks to the airport's facilities, which include restaurants, lounges, and duty-free stores. Douala International Airport, one of the busiest in Central Africa, is essential for enabling travel for both business and pleasure.

2. International airport Yaoundé Nsimalen:

Another important point of entry into Cameroon is Yaoundé Nsimalen International Airport, which is situated in the nation's capital. The infrastructure and services of this airport have been improved through extensive renovations in the last several years. Travelers using Yaoundé Nsimalen may anticipate state-of-the-art terminals, quick check-in processes, and a variety of amenities geared toward serving travelers from other countries. Because of its advantageous position, the airport is a vital hub for travelers interested in seeing Cameroon's varied landscapes and cultural attractions.

Features and Services:
Providing vital services to passengers is a top priority at both of Cameroon's international airports. These include counters for information to help with inquiries, currency exchange, and luggage management. Duty-free stores let travelers indulge in a little retail therapy before or after their flights by providing a variety of domestic and foreign goods. For luxury travelers, lounges provide a more

laid-back setting with Wi-Fi, beverages, and cozy seats.

Movement:
There are many ways to continue your journey after landing at these international airports. Travelers may easily get from Douala or Yaoundé to their selected locations with the use of taxis, shuttles, and vehicle rental services. Major cities and attractions are easily accessible from these airports because of their well-connected road networks.

COVID-19 Interventions:
In order to safeguard travelers, both airports have put strict health and safety protocols in place. Sanitation practices, social distancing guidelines, and temperature checks are a few examples of these. When arranging a trip to or from Cameroon, travelers should be aware of any current regulations pertaining to health and safety precautions.

To sum up, Cameroon's international airports are essential to the nation's global connectivity since they provide access to the many cultural, historical, and natural attractions that make this African country unique.

Internal Transit

Cameroon's domestic transportation system is a vibrant and diversified network that serves the nation's busy cities and different terrain. Traveling around Cameroon is exciting and accessible thanks to a variety of transportation options, whether you're visiting the picturesque regions of the North West or the lively streets of Douala.

1. Travel by Road:
The vast road network of Cameroon connects both distant and important towns. Shared taxis, minibuses, and buses are common forms of public transit. Buses and taxis of many colors fill the streets of major cities like Douala and Yaoundé, offering reasonably priced and practical choices for everyday transportation. "Car rapides," or long-distance buses, link major cities and provide an affordable way to travel between areas.

2. Travel by Rail:
Domestic travel in Cameroon is given a distinctive twist by the country's railway network. Important towns like Douala, Yaoundé, and Bafoussam are connected by the Camrail network, which offers a pleasant and attractive ride across the many landscapes of the nation. Because of its leisurely speed and the chance to take in breath-taking vistas of Cameroon's gorgeous countryside, train travel is especially popular.

3. Air Transportation:
Smaller regional airports make it easier to go domestically by air, which makes it a practical choice for swiftly traveling great distances. Accessible places that could be difficult to reach by car are made more accessible by the flights operated by local airlines between large cities and isolated communities. Domestic hubs, such as the airports at Douala and Yaoundé, provide frequent flights to locations all around the nation.

4. Transportation via Water:
Water transport is important in Cameroon because of its many rivers and Atlantic

coastline, particularly in the Littoral and Southwest areas. Inland rivers are navigated by traditional dugout boats, while ferry services link coastal towns. This means of transportation offers a distinctive and picturesque viewpoint of the water-rich landscapes of Cameroon.

Obstacles and Advancements:
Despite the vastness of the domestic transportation network, obstacles, including poor road conditions and sporadic interruptions, may affect travel. Infrastructure is being improved with continuing road repair projects, rail and air travel service upgrades, and other initiatives to make domestic transit more pleasant and efficient.

Moving Around Town:
Bicycle taxis and motorbike taxis, sometimes referred to as "bend-skins," are two of the many local transportation choices that cities provide to go along with their busy streets and lively marketplaces. These agile forms of transportation thread through city traffic, offering a quick and reasonably priced way to get to certain locations.

Result:
Using Cameroon's internal transportation system to see the country is an adventure in and of itself, combining beautiful scenery and cultural encounters. Every kind of transportation adds to the rich fabric of Cameroon's varied and enthralling travel experiences, from the bustling streets of large towns to the tranquil landscapes seen from trains or the distinctive canals.

Options for Local Transportation

A plethora of choices await in the colorful tapestry of Cameroon's local transportation, providing both usefulness and an unforgettable cultural experience. These local transportation options add to Cameroon's lively daily rhythm, whether it is in the country's tranquil countryside or its busy metropolitan areas.

1. Motorbike and taxi fares:
In places like Douala and Yaoundé, taxis are commonplace. They are painted in a variety of colors, each of which stands for a distinct taxi

organization. These provide a practical and reasonably priced means of navigating the bustle of the city. More nimbly options for short-distance transportation are the motorcycle taxis, sometimes referred to locally as "bend-skins," which weave through traffic. The experience is an immersion into the vibrant street culture rather than merely a way to go from point A to point B.

2. Sharing taxis and minibuses:

Minibuses, often called "bush taxis," are a common mode of transportation for short- and medium-distance trips. They provide everyday commuters with an affordable choice by operating on defined routes between towns and within cities. Similar in concept, shared taxis provide transportation to many people traveling in the same direction. These colorful cars, decked out in different decorations, capture the vibrant essence of public transit.

3. Camionettes:

Shared vans, often known as camionettes, are an additional aspect of local transportation. They connect communities and provide a vital connection for individuals who live outside of big cities, serving both rural and urban regions. Traveling in a camionette is more than simply a trip; it's a chance to converse with other travelers and exchange tales and jokes.

4. Taxis for bicycles:
Bicycle taxis serve as a substitute for other forms of transportation in certain locations, especially in smaller towns and villages. People who ride strong bikes carry people to their destinations while negotiating tight spaces and providing a greener form of transportation.

5. Conventional Boats and Canoes:
Boats that carry people across the waterways of Cameroon are an essential part of daily life for the communities located there. These water-based vehicles, which traverse rivers or sail the Atlantic coast, are essential for the movement of people and products. Gliding over the lake is akin to the intimate bond that exists between Cameroonians and their natural environment.

6. Individual Automobiles:
While public and shared modes of transportation account for the majority of local

transportation, private vehicles such as automobiles and motorcycles also play a role. These provide freedom and independence, particularly to those living in remote places with little access to public transportation.

Difficulties and Fortitude:
In Cameroon, issues with local transportation include traffic jams, poor road conditions, and even erratic scheduling. Nonetheless, the system demonstrates impressive robustness as both drivers and passengers adjust to the constantly changing nature of both urban and rural transportation.

Importance to Culture:
Beyond just being a useful means of transportation, local transportation in Cameroon is an integral part of the community. The lively chats in minivans, the shared areas in taxis, and the rhythmic buzz of motorbikes through congested streets all contribute to the vivid cultural mosaic that characterizes Cameroonians' daily lives.

To sum up, discovering Cameroon's local transportation alternatives is an immersive cultural experience rather than merely a trip.

Chapter 4

Accommodation options in Cameroon

The Best Resorts and Hotels

With its varied geography, which includes both dry savannas and lush rainforests, Cameroon is home to a number of excellent hotels and resorts that can accommodate a variety of tastes. The opulent Pullman Douala Rabingha, located in the heart of Douala, rises tall and provides a fusion of contemporary style and warm, traditional hospitality. It is a top option for business visitors because of its advantageous placement close to the economic center.

As you approach the charming city of Limbe, the Atlantic Beach Hotel becomes apparent as a waterfront treasure. Tucked away on the Atlantic Ocean's edge, this resort offers a peaceful haven with its luxurious lodgings and revitalizing spa treatments, in addition to its stunning views of the sea.

The Bimbia Bonadikombo Eco Beach Resort in Limbe is a notable choice for those looking for an environmentally conscious getaway. Nestled in the middle of the wilderness, this resort prioritizes eco-friendliness without sacrificing luxury. In eco-friendly bungalows, visitors may relax and take in the splendor of the surrounding rainforest.

As you travel north into Bamenda, you can't help but notice the striking contemporary architecture and expansive city views of the Azam Hotel & Spa. This modern hotel offers luxurious facilities and a calm atmosphere to suit both business and leisure tourists.

The Hilton Yaoundé Hotel is a towering representation of elegance and refinement in the center of the capital city of Yaoundé. Visitors can experience the city's cultural highlights thanks to its central position, and the hotel itself has a variety of culinary choices and leisure amenities.

Heading into the western highlands, Yaoundé's Mont Febe Hotel & Resort, perched on a hill, offers a tranquil haven. Encircled by an abundance of vegetation, this hotel provides a serene setting for those looking for a quiet getaway.

Though these are just a few instances, Cameroon's varied topography is matched by an assortment of lodging options, each providing a distinctive experience. Cameroon has something for every kind of tourist, whether they are more interested in a hidden natural sanctuary or the hustle and bustle of the metropolis.

Affordable Accommodations

Budget-conscious tourists visiting Cameroon may find a variety of reasonably priced but cozy lodging options dispersed around the nation. The Hotel Franco, located in the center of Yaoundé, is an affordable choice with straightforward, spotless rooms that don't sacrifice necessary conveniences. For visitors who want to see the city's highlights without going over budget, its central location is ideal.

Relocating to Douala, the Ibis Douala is an inexpensive chain hotel that provides dependable lodging at reasonable prices. With its uncomplicated approach to hospitality, it offers guests who appreciate value an affordable stay.

For a more leisurely experience, the Mermoz Hotel in Limbe provides reasonably priced accommodations in a laid-back atmosphere. Tucked away from the bustle, it's a great option for anyone looking for an affordable, serene getaway that's still close to the city's attractions.

The Ayaba Hotel in Bamenda offers reasonably priced lodging without sacrificing comfort. It is a good option for low-cost visitors who want to see the quaint town and its surroundings because of its inviting attitude and advantageous location.

Budget lodging with an emphasis on sustainability is available at the Green Valley Hotel in Buea for individuals who have a thing for environmentally conscious travel. The hotel's dedication to ecological standards is a good fit for budget-minded, environmentally conscious tourists.

The Hotel Residence La Falaise in Garoua offers reasonably priced lodging in the northern region of Cameroon, ideal for seeing the country's varied landscapes. Its simple yet cozy accommodations satisfy budget-conscious guests without compromising on basic conveniences.

Cameroon offers a variety of possibilities for low-cost travel, thanks to its diverse cultural heritage and stunning natural surroundings. These reasonably priced accommodations guarantee that you may take in Cameroon's splendor without breaking the bank, whether you want to stay in bustling cities or tranquil countryside.

Special Accommodations and Sustainable Choices

With its varied ecosystems and dedication to environmental preservation, Cameroon provides visitors with a distinctive selection of accommodations that uphold eco-friendly standards. The Nyong Palace Hotel in Ebolowa is a noteworthy choice, as it skillfully combines traditional architecture with eco-friendly living. Encircled by verdant gardens, this ecologically conscious sanctuary offers a cultural experience and supports eco-friendly activities, making it a perfect option for tourists who care about the environment.

The Rhino Resort Hotel & Spa in Akonolinga is a standout choice for a memorable stay. With undulating hills as a background, this resort emphasizes peaceful cohabitation with nature by incorporating eco-friendly techniques into its operations and design. Visitors may enjoy the resort's dedication to sustainability while losing themselves in a peaceful setting.

Les Gites de Kribi, located in the seaside village of Kribi, provides a distinctive fusion of traditional thatched-roof bungalows with environmentally conscious methods. Tucked away on the Atlantic coast, this eco-lodge places a strong emphasis on eco-friendly travel, giving visitors a chance to get in touch with the natural world while leaving as little of an environmental impact as possible.

The Ekom Nkam Waterfall Lodge, located deep among Cameroon's beautiful rainforests, provides an incredibly unique experience. Located next to the well-known Ekom Nkam Waterfall, this eco-friendly resort lets visitors take part in environmentally responsible activities like bird viewing and guided nature walks while also fully immersing them in the natural beauty of the area.

A unique place to stay for people looking for a treehouse adventure is the Tree House at the Limbe Wildlife Centre. Situated within the animal refuge, visitors may enjoy high treehouse lodgings with views and sounds of the tropical jungle all around them. This environmentally responsible decision benefits the Limbe Wildlife Centre's conservation work in addition to offering a great vacation.

These particular accommodations, which emphasize both the preservation of the rich natural heritage of the nation and the provision of a unique experience, are a prime example of Cameroon's dedication to sustainable tourism. Travelers are looking for eco-friendly lodgings more and more, and these hotels highlight Cameroon's commitment to providing distinctive, sustainable, and immersive experiences.

Chapter 5

Exploring Yaoundé- the Capital City

Historical Landmarks

Cameroon has an extensive collection of historical sites that attest to its rich cultural legacy and turbulent history. The Bimbia Slave Trade Port, which is located on the Atlantic coast, is one such site. This eerie location offers a window into Cameroon's dark past and a sobering reminder of the country's role in the transatlantic slave trade.

As one moves inland, one finds the Tikar people's royal palaces, which are both architectural wonders and cultural riches. These palaces, which are situated in Cameroon's grasslands, shed light on the customary social structures and governing practices of the Tikar people. These constructions' elaborate workmanship and symbolic components are a reflection of their profound cultural value, which has endured throughout centuries.

As one travels farther, the Rhumsiki Peak becomes apparent as a natural marvel and evidence of Cameroon's diverse geological makeup. This famous volcanic plug, which has been shaped by the elements for millennia, provides amazing sweeping views of the Mandara Mountains in the vicinity. Beyond its geological importance, it is also a spiritual location for the indigenous Kapsiki people, who perform customary rites under its shadow.

A UNESCO World Heritage Site, the Dja Faunal Reserve demonstrates Cameroon's dedication to the preservation of wildlife. A stunning variety of flora and animals, including uncommon species like forest elephants and chimpanzees, may be found in this virgin jungle. The reserve emphasizes the need to protect these habitats for future generations in addition to acting as a monument to Cameroon's biological diversity.

The Independence Monument is located in the center of Yaoundé, the capital city of Cameroon. The monument, which was built to honor the nation's 1960 independence from French and British colonial authority, represents the tenacity and ambitions of the Cameroonian people. Its design includes components that express the unity of the country and its will to pave its own course.

Exploring Cameroon's historical sites reveals that each location contributes to the mosaic of the country's identity by weaving a distinct story. Cameroon's monuments convey stories of the past while also acting as beacons, pointing the country toward a future influenced by its rich legacy. These beacons may be heard in the solemn echoes of the Bimbia Slave Trade Port or in the vivid colors of cultural expression found in the Royal Palaces.

Institutions of Culture

Numerous cultural organizations exist in Cameroon, a nation with a wide range of nationalities and traditions, and they look after the rich legacy of the country. The Cameroon Cultural Center in Yaoundé is one of the most notable of them as a center for creative expression and cross-cultural interaction. Through its exhibits, seminars, and events, this organization fosters modern innovation while simultaneously playing a crucial role in the preservation of traditional arts, crafts, and performances.

Another important component of Cameroon's cultural environment is the National Museum of Yaoundé. Its vast collection includes modern artworks, ethnographic exhibits, and items from archaeology. As a treasure trove, the museum takes guests on a trip through the history of the nation, from pre-colonial times to the present, providing insights into the many cultures and traditions that help to define Cameroon's character.

The Bamoun Sultan's Palace at Foumban, a symbol of the Bamoun people's artistic and architectural skill, is a significant cultural landmark. This palace, which is full of colorful decorations and detailed carvings, is not only the home of the traditional monarch but also a living museum that displays the customs and history of the dynasty.

Organizations such as the Bandjoun Museum demonstrate Cameroon's dedication to maintaining linguistic and cultural variety. Established by the well-known artist Barthélémy Toguo, this organization honors the Bamileke people's cultural legacy. It serves as a venue for modern artists to investigate and reinterpret their cultural origins, in addition to serving as a place for the exhibition of traditional objects.

The Douala Art and Culture Center is one of the cultural establishments that serve as a home to Cameroon's thriving music industry. This vibrant venue not only supports regional artists and musicians but also welcomes international partnerships, resulting in a mash-up of musical influences that reflects the nation's openness to international cultural exchange.

The Etonnants Voyageurs Festival in Saint-Louis provides a forum for authors and scholars to participate in conversations on literature, culture, and society. By presenting the writings of both local and foreign writers, this literary institution not only promotes a sense of intellectual community but also adds to Cameroon's literary environment.

Together, these cultural institutions add to Cameroon's tapestry of cultures, strengthening the nation's sense of identity and community. These institutions are essential to creating and maintaining the rich cultural mosaic that characterizes Cameroon, whether via traditional art forms, modern manifestations, or thought-provoking dialogue.

Street life and local markets

Exploring the vibrant local markets of Cameroon offers a sensory journey into the very core of the nation. These colorful markets, which can be found all throughout towns and cities, are teeming with people going about their everyday lives and are full of color and activity. The Mfoundi Market in Yaoundé is one such famous market; it is a kaleidoscope of booths showcasing Cameroon's vibrant street life and wide variety of commodities.

The marketplaces come alive with the colorful colors of traditional garments, the symphony of spices, and the rhythmic cadence of haggling as the sun sets. Like many other markets, Mfoundi Market develops as a hub for the exchange of commodities and tales among residents from all backgrounds.

From vibrant displays of fruits like plantains and mangoes to exotic spices that fill the air with their alluring scent, the booths are a veritable gold mine of fresh products. Handmade products, from traditional wooden carvings to delicately woven baskets, are proudly displayed by local artists. Each item tells a story of the creator's cultural history and skill.

These marketplaces' accompanying street life is just as fascinating. Makeshift booths litter the narrow passageways, each providing a different window into the everyday lives of Cameroonians. Vendors exhibit a remarkable range of products, including handcrafted jewelry and regional foods, while they deftly balance baskets on their heads. These busy streets are accompanied by a dynamic symphony created by the sounds of laughter, lively conversations, and the sporadic calls of street merchants.

The ambiance changes in the evenings when street food merchants open their stalls and tempt onlookers with the fragrance of grilled meats spiced with a variety of spices. Families and friends congregate around impromptu tables to enjoy the tastes of regional specialties, generating a feeling of camaraderie that is fundamental to Cameroon's street culture. This fosters a community attitude.

Discovering the local marketplaces and engaging with Cameroonian street life is an intimate trip into the community's heart rather than just a commercial experience. It is a site where the nation's heart beats, customs are preserved, and the tenacity, variety, and unwavering spirit of the Cameroonian people are interwoven into the colorful fabric of everyday life.

Chapter 6

Discovering Douala—the Economic Center

Port City and Economic Hub

Located on the Gulf of Guinea, Douala is the capital and largest port city of Cameroon, combining traditional culture with modern trade. With its throbbing vitality, this dynamic city acts as the nation's commercial hub, promoting economic expansion and global commerce.

A wide range of sectors, like manufacturing, services, and finance, define Douala's economic environment. Its advantageous position as a port city, which makes it easier to import and export commodities and connects Cameroon to international markets, greatly enhances its economic strength. With its sophisticated infrastructure and role as a gateway for international commerce, the busy port of Douala plays a crucial role in the economic dynamics of the area.

The autonomous port authority is in charge of the Port of Douala, which is essential to the city's economic system. It can handle a wide range of cargo, from consumer products to industrial gear, and can accommodate a multitude of boats. Cameroon's economic resilience is bolstered by the port's efficiency and capacity, which facilitate the smooth flow of commodities and improve the country's trade competitiveness.

Douala's economic vitality goes beyond its marine importance to its position as a finance center. A thriving financial ecosystem is supported by the city's concentration of banks, financial institutions, and investment enterprises. This concentration of financial institutions has elevated Douala to the forefront of Cameroon's economic scene by attracting international investment and supporting local enterprises.

The city's industrial sector also contributes to its economic significance. Douala is home to factories that make a wide variety of goods, including processed foods and textiles. In addition to creating job opportunities, this industrial diversification boosts the country's ability to export and be self-sufficient.

Douala's commercial districts, business centers, and lively marketplaces are all strewn across the city, giving the city an economic pulse that is closely linked to its urban fabric. The steady hum of business activity is indicative of Douala's economy's flexibility and tenacity as it overcomes obstacles and seizes development possibilities.

To sum up, Douala is proof of the mutually beneficial link that exists between economic dynamism and a flourishing port city. Its advantageous location and varied economic environment make it a vital component of Cameroon's progress toward long-term development and international integration.

Entertainment and the Waterfront

The coastline and entertainment district of Douala combine to create a mesmerizing tapestry that showcases the cultural diversity of the city and offers a comfortable space for relaxation and mingling. The waterfront, which stretches along the Wouri River, is a beloved location for both residents and tourists because it provides a lovely setting for a variety of leisure pursuits and entertainment options.

Douala's waterfront is more than simply a geographical location; it's a cultural center where the rhythmic flow of the river and the pulse of the city collide. One is engulfed in a sensory experience that embodies Douala's lively atmosphere as they stroll down the promenade. The beautiful combination created by the contemporary buildings set against the scenic riverbank symbolizes the city's growth while paying tribute to its historical heritage.

With its array of cafés, restaurants, and outdoor markets, the riverside boulevard provides a wide variety of gastronomic experiences. Whether enjoying exotic cuisines or local specialties, eating by the seaside offers an entire dining experience in addition to a meal. Enjoying a meal while taking in the expansive views of the river and the Douala cuisine while being lulled by the tranquil sounds of the flowing water is a memorable experience.

As varied as the city itself, the entertainment alternatives available along the waterfront. The riverfront transforms into a vibrant platform for creative expression, hosting anything from outdoor live music events to cultural festivals honoring Cameroon's rich history. An ambiance that speaks to the city's multicultural character is created by fusing modern sounds with ancient rhythms.

Boat trips on the Wouri River provide visitors and locals with a unique viewpoint of Douala, enabling them to see the city's skyline while they float on the calm currents. Sunset excursions, in particular, turn the shoreline into an orange and pink painting that captivates the senses, offering a peaceful and romantic experience.

In addition, the waterfront acts as a gathering place for individuals of all ages looking to unwind and have fun. Amidst the river, families congregate for picnics, lovers stroll romantically, and friends have lively discussions. The waterfront creates a sense of community that makes it a social area where shared experiences turn into enduring memories.

Douala's waterfront and entertainment options, taken together, characterize the city's leisure activities in a dynamic way. It's a location where the Wouri River's natural beauty meets the cultural richness and inventiveness of its people, providing a unique experience that makes a lasting impression on those who are lucky enough to visit this enchanted haven of leisure and pleasure.

The Scene of Culinary Arts

The gourmet trip that is Douala's culinary scene reflects the city's rich cultural tapestry, enticing the senses with a wide variety of tastes and culinary customs. Douala's culinary scene reflects the blending of regional products, global influences, and a deep-seated love for culinary talent, from lively street markets to elegant dining venues.

Douala's marketplaces, including Marché Sandaga, are lively gathering places where the city's rich gastronomic variety is shown. A kaleidoscope of fresh vegetables, fragrant spices, and unusual ingredients may be found among the market booths, producing a sensory symphony that encapsulates Cameroon's culinary legacy. Dishes like Ndolé, Sanga-sanga, and Poulet DG, which highlight the richness and depth of Cameroonian cuisine, are expertly crafted by local merchants.

Douala's culinary scene is particularly known for its street cuisine, with food carts and roadside vendors serving a wide variety of delicious treats. A local favorite, grilled fish sizzles over open flames, filling the air with enticing scents. Enjoying a bowl of hot Achu or Mbanga soup from the street transforms dining into an immersive cultural experience that gives a flavor of Douala's dynamic street food scene.

Douala has a growing scene of restaurants that combine history and innovation for those looking for a more sophisticated dining experience. Fine dining establishments in the city center or along the seaside are gastronomic havens where chefs expertly transform regional ingredients into delectable dishes. World cuisines coexist peacefully with traditional Cameroonian fare, offering a gastronomic adventure suitable for a wide range of tastes.

Given its seaside position, the city is known for its love affair with seafood, and there are plenty of seafood restaurants serving a wide variety of fresh catches. Douala's waterfront eating facilities provide a convivial ambiance while serving up delicacies from the Atlantic Ocean, such as beautifully cooked lobster, shrimp, and a variety of fish.

Furthermore, Douala's café culture gives the city's food scene a refined touch. Around the city are hip bakeries and coffee shops that provide a delicious selection of pastries, specialty coffees, and desserts. These places, which often double as cultural centers, provide residents with a place to relax, socialize, and savor the subtler aspects of Douala's developing food scene.

Douala's cuisine is essentially a celebration of variety, a well-balanced fusion of local specialties with cutting-edge innovation. Every dish on this gastronomic journey tells a tale, and each meal turns into an investigation of a different culture. Douala's culinary options are a tribute to the city's culinary expertise and its people's appreciation for excellent food and shared experiences, from the busy markets to the posh eating venues.

Chapter 7

Natural Wonders in Cameroon

Discovering Mount Cameroon

Mount Cameroon is a beautiful sentinel that dominates the terrain, nestled on the western tip of Central Africa. This stratovolcano, which rises to a height of around 4,040 meters (13,255 feet), attracts attention with its utter majesty and natural charm.

The dense rainforests that cover the mountain's lower slopes eventually give way to rocky terrain and alpine meadows as one gets closer to the summit. The ascent is a captivating progression through a variety of habitats, each of which displays a distinctive mosaic of flora and wildlife.

The colorful symphony of tropical animals reverberates on the slopes of Mount Cameroon. The lower altitudes are covered in dense, biologically rich woods that provide a refuge for a wide variety of plant and animal species. The smell of wet ground and the echoing cries of far-off birds fill the air.

The terrain changes as one ascends higher in height. One comes across a range of indigenous plant species that have adapted to the colder climate while climbing through highland forests. Trees covered in moss provide a magical ambiance, while vibrant orchids often cover the ground, softening the harsh climb.

As one approaches the alpine zone, the flora thins down and is replaced by rugged bushes and steep hillsides. The air is fresh here, and expansive vistas stretch out in all directions. The climb becomes harder, with each step demanding fortitude and will in the face of the dwindling air.

A stunning overview of the surrounding landscape can be seen from the peak of Mount Cameroon. The Atlantic Ocean shimmers in the distance on clear days, offering a striking contrast to the untamed landscape below. The peak's caldera displays the dormant volcano's geological past, providing insight into the processes that sculpted this amazing terrain.

For those who take on the task, climbing Mount Cameroon offers a deep spiritual connection with the natural world in addition to a physical test. It's an investigation of ecosystems, an aerial dance, and an acknowledgment of the innate beauty that Mother Nature has created over millions of years. A sensation of wonder and achievement permeates the air as you stand atop Mount Cameroon, surrounded by its untamed wildness.

Waza National Park

Waza National Park is tucked away in Cameroon's northern regions, where it spreads out like a wild, undeveloped painting. This ecological sanctuary, which covers an area of more than 1,700 square kilometers, is evidence of the nation's dedication to protecting its natural heritage. Entering the center of Waza, the terrain reveals a beautiful mosaic of varied environments, ranging from vast savannahs to meandering riverbanks.

An incredible variety of species finds refuge in the park, which is a monument to the delicate balance of nature. Elephants are free to explore the wide meadows, their elegant shapes contrasting with the savannah's golden tones. The untamed spirit of the African bush is personified by lions, elusive and magnificent creatures who pursue their prey in the dense grass.

The park's appeal to ornithologists is enhanced by the presence of birds in Waza. The sounds of many different bird species, including the well-known African fish eagle and the vibrant plumage of lilac-breasted rollers, fill the air. Waza is a birder's paradise, providing an opportunity to see the beautiful dance of feathers and songs in their native environment.

The park's flowing Waza River provides vitality for the varied plant and animal species. A vibrant ecology teeming with life is created by hippos submerging themselves in the cold waters and crocodiles lounging in the sun along the banks. The riverbanks turn into a natural theatrical theater where prey and predators perform a never-ending dance of survival.

As one travels more into Waza, they come across settlements of people whose lives are woven together with the patterns of the natural environment. Across the vast plains, nomadic herders lead their livestock in a mutually beneficial partnership that has persisted for many centuries. The peace that results from local residents and animals coexisting on the same stage is shown.

Waza National Park is more than just a place to visit; it is evidence of the careful balancing act that occurs between nature and mankind. Here, where the sounds of the wild, the rustle of the grass, and the wind all combine to create Africa's pulse, it stands as a beacon of conservation. Discovering Waza is an all-encompassing voyage into Cameroon's spirit, one that leaves lasting impressions of wonder and admiration for the beauty that abounds in the center of the continent.

The Botanical Garden of Limbe

The Limbe Botanic Garden, which is located in southwest Cameroon and is tucked away along the picturesque Atlantic Ocean coast, is a lush oasis that stands as a tribute to the abundant biodiversity that exists in this region of Africa. This 53-hectare botanical sanctuary is more than simply a garden; it's a living encyclopedia of the variety of plants that exist in Cameroon.

A feeling of peace permeates the senses as soon as one steps foot in the Limbe Botanic Garden. The thick foliage offers a nice break from the busyness of the outside world, and the air is fragrant with the subtle scents of exotic blossoms. With great care and attention to detail, the garden protects rare and endangered plant species while also preserving the area's natural history.

As guests walk around the garden's winding paths, they come upon an enthralling assortment of flora, with each species carefully identified, providing an informative tour of

Cameroon's botanical treasures. Dappled shadows are formed on the ground below by the tall trees that form a canopy above, their branches entwining to form a natural cathedral that screens the sunshine.

The Limbe Botanic Garden is a dynamic living laboratory rather than just a static exhibit of plants. Globally renowned botanists and researchers gather here to investigate and preserve the wide variety of plant species that call Cameroon home. Beyond the garden's boundaries, conservation initiatives support the larger goal of protecting the nation's distinctive ecosystems.

The Orchid House, a mesmerizing haven where colorful orchids—some of which are native to the area—bloom in a blaze of color, is a garden highlight. It's a sensory extravaganza where the exquisite beauty of these exotic flowers enthralls guests and emphasizes how crucial it is to preserve such sensitive ecosystems.

The garden serves as a focal point for environmental education and community involvement, in addition to being a site for scientific research. Students from nearby schools are often brought to Limbe, which helps establish a link between the next generation and the value of biodiversity preservation. An immersive experience is created via workshops, guided tours, and interactive displays, which provide a greater understanding of the complex web of life that grows inside the garden's boundaries.

The Limbe Botanic Garden is a live example of how humans and the environment are intertwined, not only a display of Cameroon's botanical diversity. It leaves a lasting mark of respect for nature by inviting visitors to investigate, discover, and consider the fragility and resilience of our planet's ecosystems.

Chapter 8

Cameroon Cultural Immersion

Traditional Festivals

The ethnic diversity of Cameroon's people is reflected in the country's rich tapestry of traditional celebrations. These celebrations are lively representations of cultural identity and legacy because they are firmly anchored in the traditions and beliefs of diverse groups.

The Ngondo Festival, an important occasion for the Duala people living near the shore, is one notable festival. This festival honors the spirits of the ocean and is centered on marine customs. It is held annually in Douala, the country's commercial center. The Duala community celebrates the anniversary with elaborate celebrations that include vibrant processions, traditional dances, and symbolic rites. These activities help to strengthen the group's sense of continuity and solidarity.

The Bamoun people celebrate the Nguon Festival with tremendous fervor farther north. This celebration, which is centered in Foumban, the Bamoun kingdom's cultural center, is a mesmerizing exhibition of royal pomp and ceremony. The royal parade, which features the kingdom's historical relics and cultural riches, is the main event. It is headed by the Fon, the traditional monarch. The celebrations are made more mysterious by the elaborate masquerades, music, and traditional dances.

The Kom people celebrate the Nso' Festival in the Western Highlands, which emphasizes the importance of agricultural methods. This celebration highlights the social bonds that unite the Nso' people via vibrant displays of traditional clothing and complex dance performances. In addition, it provides a stage for paying respect to the spirits of the ancestors and requesting their blessings for a bumper crop.

The Bali Nyonga people celebrate the Nguon Festival, which is a reflection of their agricultural heritage, as they move eastward. The community of Bali Nyonga hosts the event, which includes a number of customs, including symbolic seed sowing and traditional dances that represent the natural cycles. The community asks for heavenly favor for successful agricultural seasons and shows thanks for the land's fertility via these ceremonies.

The festivals of Cameroon are an important means of passing down customs from one generation to the next, in addition to honoring the country's rich cultural legacy. These celebrations are essential to maintaining and strengthening the distinctive traditions that make up Cameroon's diverse cultural landscape as the country develops.

Native American groups

Nestled in the heart of Africa, Cameroon is home to a diverse range of indigenous people, each with its own unique customs, cultural practices, and ways of life. These settlements add to the rich cultural mix of the country, dispersed across its many geographic settings.

The Bakas are one such tribe that lives in the southeast's deep jungles. Adhering to a distinct style of nomadic hunting and gathering, the Bakas live in perfect peace with the natural world. Their deep understanding of the forest serves as both a survival strategy and a cultural legacy that is handed down through the ages. They celebrate their cultural identity and have a strong connection with the environment, which is shown in the importance of traditional music and dance in their social fabric.

The grasslands and savannas of Cameroon are traversed by the pastoralist Mbororo people, who live in nomadic groups. The Mbororo, who are well-known for their vibrant clothing and unique jewelry, have a rich oral tradition that captures their culture, history, and collective knowledge. Their primary source of income is cattle raising, and their nomadic way of life demonstrates a mutually beneficial connection with the land and its resources.

The Bamileke people, who live mostly in the Western Highlands, are renowned for their vivid beading, beautiful woodcarvings, and extravagant festivities. The Bamileke practice traditional skills, weaving, and agriculture while placing a high priority on community ideals. The chieftaincy system and the design of their palaces emphasize the importance of social structure and governance in their society.

The Fulbe, also called the Fulani, are a dominant group in the northern areas. The Fulbe people are mostly pastoralists who travel over the Sahelian regions with their herds, representing a nomadic way of life that is strongly embedded in their cultural ethos. The Fulbe are renowned for their unique kinds of cattle and intricate cuisine made entirely of milk. They also have a strong oral culture that is conveyed via music, storytelling, and poetry.

One of the oldest indigenous communities is the Bagyeli, who live in the southern Cameroonian jungles. The Bagyeli have a special affinity with the forest ecosystem and engage in customary hunting and gathering while preserving a spiritual connection with their environment. Their deep familiarity with therapeutic plants and responsible resource management emphasize their stewardship of the forest.

These indigenous groups greatly enhance Cameroon's cultural diversity with their varied languages, traditions, and belief systems. To ensure that these indigenous communities' rich tapestry continues to weave through the fabric of Cameroon's cultural identity, efforts to conserve and celebrate their legacy are more important as the country struggles with modernity and globalization.

Language and Communication

Cameroon is notable for its intriguing mosaic of dialects and communication patterns. Cameroon's linguistic landscape, with more than 250 ethnic groupings, each with its own distinct language or dialect, is evidence of the nation's rich cultural legacy.

The two official languages of Cameroon, French and English, are fundamental to this linguistic variety and are a holdover from the country's colonial past. This bilingualism, also referred to as "le bilinguisme," is present in many areas of everyday life, including media, trade, and administration, as well as education. These two European languages coexist in a delicate equilibrium that protects the linguistic sovereignty of many ethnic populations while still promoting a feeling of national unity.

In addition to the official languages, Cameroon is home to several indigenous languages that enrich the linguistic mosaic that characterizes each community. The linguistic landscape of the country is a mosaic, reflecting the cultural variety of the country, with Bantu languages spoken in the south and Afro-Asiatic languages spoken in the north. The worldviews of speakers of different languages are influenced by their respective historical, social, and environmental backgrounds.

Apart from verbal communication, Cameroon also values nonverbal forms such as complex hand signals, music, and traditional dance. These nonverbal cues are effective ways to communicate stories, feelings, and a sense of group belonging. Weddings and funerals are examples of traditional rites that often include expressive dances and rituals that convey deep cultural importance.

Furthermore, with the widespread use of mobile phones and internet access, the modern age has brought forth new dynamics in communication. Through the use of social media and digital communication technologies, Cameroonians are now able to interact and exchange experiences with people from a variety of linguistic backgrounds, overcoming obstacles posed by distance and language.

However, linguistic variety is also threatened by the quick speed of industrialization. Since younger generations are more likely to utilize official languages like English or other global lingua franca, several indigenous languages are in danger of disappearing. Indigenous language promotion and preservation activities include educational campaigns, cultural events, and oral tradition documentation.

Essentially, Cameroon's language mosaic depicts the complex relationship between tradition and modernity. Indigenous dialects, official languages, and nonverbal communication styles coexist in a complex tapestry that demonstrates the country's cultural adaptation and durability. Celebrating and protecting this variety is essential to Cameroon's cultural identity as it continues to negotiate its linguistic terrain.

Chapter 9

Outdoor Activities and Adventure

Trekking and Hiking

Hiking and trekking across Cameroon's beautiful landscapes reveals a tapestry of natural marvels where lively cultures, towering mountains, and lush rainforests combine. The vast diversity of this African nation's geography becomes apparent as you travel throughout it, providing outdoor enthusiasts with a special mix of rewards and difficulties.

As the tallest mountain in West Africa, the picturesque Mount Cameroon beckons adventurous climbers to ascend its slopes. The breathtaking views from the peak, where the Atlantic Ocean meets the Cameroon Highlands, are an unmatched sight, but the trek is a test of mental and physical toughness. A taste of the natural variety that characterizes Cameroon is offered by the several habitats seen throughout the ascent, which range from deep rainforests to alpine meadows.

Going beyond Mount Cameroon, the Mandara Mountains' Kapsiki Peaks provide a different view. Trekking over the Kapsiki Plateau demonstrates the unwavering vitality of local inhabitants by revealing magnificent rock formations and historic towns teetering on cliff edges. Interacting with Cameroonian culture enhances the hiking experience by bringing a sense of the interdependence of human existence and the natural world to the native people.

Another treasure for hikers is the UNESCO Biosphere Reserve, Waza National Park. Trekkers that make their way over this enormous area are exposed to the rich biodiversity of the Sahel region, where they may see giraffes, elephants, and a wide variety of bird species. The park's many habitats, which range from marshes to savannas, provide visitors with an immersive experience that emphasizes how crucial conservation efforts are to maintaining Cameroon's natural legacy.

One cannot overlook the friendliness and generosity of the Cameroonian people throughout these hiking and trekking experiences. Local guides, who often have a close connection with the land, impart tales that shed light on the region's diverse cultural landscape in addition to their expertise on the trails. The hiking experience is enhanced by traditional dances, music, and food, which transcend beyond the actual terrain.

In conclusion, Cameroonian hiking and trekking combine the richness of cross-cultural experiences with the difficulties of the environment to create a story of adventure. Along with beautiful views, the pathways let hikers gain a deep understanding of the symbiotic interaction that exists between this African treasure's different habitats and its inhabitants. With every step of this journey, a new chapter opens up, and Cameroon proves to be an enthralling location for travelers looking for an intense and life-changing outdoor experience.

Safaris with wildlife

Going on a wildlife safari in Cameroon is like entering a documentary where the raw beauty of the natural world is the main focus. This West African treasure's many ecosystems provide a kaleidoscope of flora and animals, making for an immersive safari experience that is unmatched anywhere else in the world.

The Waza National Park is a popular spot for wildlife aficionados, offering a refuge for those hoping to get up close and personal with some of Africa's most recognizable animals. Large savannas in the park provide giraffes, elephants, lions, and many other animals with a natural home. Visitors may see the captivating sight of wild animals up close while exploring the park's network of trails by jeep or on foot. This illustrates the precarious balance between predator and prey in this biodiverse region.

With almost 900 bird species identified, Cameroon is a veritable gold mine for avian enthusiasts. Observing a variety of vibrant and secretive bird species in their native environment is a rare experience provided by the Dja Faunal Reserve, a UNESCO World Heritage Site. Birding aficionados will find this region's lush rainforests to be a mesmerizing setting, with a symphony of nature created by the melodies of various bird cries.

A journey into the center of Lobeke National Park demonstrates the close relationship that exists between people and animals. One of the remaining hunter-gatherer cultures in Africa, the Baka people, still live in this park, which exemplifies sustainable cohabitation with the natural world. Safari visitors get the opportunity to see age-old hunting methods that have been handed down through the centuries, providing a window into the complex interactions that exist between native populations and the wildlife that coexists in their area.

The Atlantic coast's Campo Ma'an National Park gives the wildlife safari experience a sea element. Sea turtles and a variety of bird species may be seen against the background of mangrove swamps, coastal woodlands, and immaculate beaches. This park's juxtaposition of terrestrial and marine habitats serves as an example of Cameroon's dedication to biodiversity protection due to its natural richness.

The Limbe Wildlife Centre, which specializes in the rehabilitation and preservation of primates, is another example of Cameroon's dedication to conservation. Guests may gain an understanding of the difficulties associated with animal conservation in the area by directly seeing the efforts made to save endangered species, such as gorillas and chimpanzees.

Essentially, a wildlife safari in Cameroon is an expedition that envelops visitors in the complex web of life, in which every species plays a crucial function, rather than just a trip through environments rich with unusual creatures. It's a chance to take in the raw beauty of the natural world, to recognize the exquisite balance that supports a variety of ecosystems, and to support the continuous efforts to protect the great diversity of species that characterizes this fascinating country in Africa.

Water-Based Adventures

Discovering Cameroon's water activities is like setting off on a voyage that reveals a variety of aquatic marvels, from calm river cruises to thrilling white-water rafting. The many rivers that wind through this country in West Africa provide a playground for swimmers looking for calm as well as heart-pounding excitement.

The Sanaga River provides a serene environment for river trips as it meanders through the center of Cameroon. Visitors may fully immerse themselves in the beautiful surroundings while canoeing along its calm currents. The experience is well balanced with the natural world, with lively birds and the odd sighting of hippos. The contemplative quality of Sanaga's slow cadence provides a welcome diversion from the hectic pace of daily living.

The challenge of white-water rafting on the Nkam River is there for those who are looking for even more adrenaline. This watercourse's twists and bends, together with its rushing rapids, provide for an exhilarating ride where managing the turbulent waters requires expertise and collaboration. For those looking for an exhilarating experience in Cameroon, the white-water adventure is a must-try because of the breathtaking scenery that complements the heart-pounding excitement.

Another aspect of aquatic experiences may be found along the Atlantic coast, where Limbe is a prominent center for marine activities. The spot is perfect for snorkeling and scuba diving because of the immaculate beaches and crystal-clear seas. Discovering the beautiful underwater world offers a captivating experience below the surface as coral reefs brimming with colorful fish and other marine life are revealed.

Kayaking and boating may be enjoyed against the unusual background of Lake Nyos, a volcanic crater lake tucked away in the foothills. The lake's placid waters and verdant surroundings provide for a tranquil setting ideal for unhurried exploration. The haunting past of Lake Nyos, which was the scene of a terrible natural tragedy in the 1980s, highlights the dynamic forces of nature that sculpt Cameroon's landscapes and lends an air of intrigue to the aquatic experience.

The Manengouba twin lakes, located farther inland, provide an enthralling environment for water-based adventures. These lakes, which are surrounded by undulating hills and deep woods, provide a beautiful setting for fishing and kayaking. For those looking for a more introspective aquatic experience, the peace and quiet of the surrounding area combined with the placid calm of the lakes make an ideal haven.

To put it simply, Cameroonian water adventures go above and beyond the norm, providing a wide range of activities to suit every kind of aquatic need. Adventurers are invited to explore the beauty and thrill that lie beyond the surface of Cameroon's rivers, whether it's by relaxing on a tranquil river, racing down a white-water raft, or diving into underwater worlds.

Chapter 10

Historical and Cultural Sites

Foumban's Royal Palace

Located in the center of Cameroon, Foumban's Royal Palace is a testimony to the rich cultural legacy and history of the Bamoun people. Rich in history, this architectural wonder is both a tangible representation of the Bamoun monarchy and a storehouse of the colorful past of the area.

Built under Sultan Njoya's rule in the early 1900s, the palace has a distinctive fusion of native architectural forms that capture the essence of the Bamoun people's culture. Its elaborate design, which is distinguished by elaborate carvings and vivid colors, is a visual feast that transports guests back in time.

You can't help but be in awe of the artistry on display in every nook and cranny of the palace as you make your way through its vast courtyards and winding hallways. Every feature, from the intricate woodwork decorating entrances to the symbolic symbols gracing the walls, tells a tale that is firmly ingrained in the history and beliefs of the Bamoun people.

The palace's interior rooms display the grandeur and dignity typical of the Bamoun nobility. The throne chamber offers an insight into the rites and ceremonies that have taken place within its walls throughout the ages. It is furnished with royal furniture and ceremonial items. A strong link between the past and present is made possible by the royal artifacts on exhibit, which provide an insight into the traditions and customs of the Bamoun people.

In addition to being an important architectural landmark, Foumban's Royal Palace is a dynamic example of the Bamoun people's tenacity. The palace endures the test of time, serving as a reminder of the Bamoun kingdom's lasting heritage and a source of cultural pride. For anyone looking to fully immerse themselves in the rich tapestry of Cameroon's history and cultural heritage, it continues to be a must-visit location.

The cultural heritage of Bamenda

Nestled in the picturesque Northwestern Highlands of Cameroon, Bamenda is a cultural treasure trove that enthralls tourists with its rich history and various customs. The habits and practices of the many ethnic groups that inhabit this area are woven into the cultural fabric of Bamenda, producing a lively mosaic that represents unity in variety.

The Grassfield people have had a significant impact on Bamenda's cultural legacy, having been instrumental in forming the region's customs. Every facet of everyday life is infused with a feeling of cultural pride, from the colorful dances that fill the air during joyful festivals to the skilled beading and textile arts that decorate ceremonial apparel.

The recognizable Nso Palace guards the cultural importance of Bamenda. Constructed in the

14th century, this architectural wonder is a living museum of NSO history as well as a physical building. Its elaborate carvings, ancestor items, and hallowed areas provide a window into the rites and rituals that have long been important to the Nso people.

The vibrant cultural life of Bamenda is further enhanced by its lively marketplaces. Here, the colors of traditional textiles blend with the perfume of regional specialties to create a sensory experience that captures the vibrant energy of the neighborhood. In addition, the markets act as gathering places for the inhabitants, promoting a feeling of togetherness and community that is essential to Bamenda's cultural fabric.

Two essential elements of Bamenda culture are music and dancing. Through the hills reverberate traditional rhythms and songs, often accompanied by native instruments, telling tales of victory, love, and ancient knowledge. Every year, the Bamenda Traditional Dance Festival serves as a platform for these vibrant cultural manifestations, attracting attendees and performers from all across the area.

You can't help but get engrossed in the rich cultural tapestry that characterizes this alluring area as you travel through Bamenda's terrain, whether it is via the charming highlands or the busy metropolitan centers. Bamenda's cultural history is dynamic and ever-changing, influencing the identity of its people and inviting outsiders to discover the many sides of its customs. It is not something that is stuck in the past.

People's artifacts from Tikar

The wonderful items of the Tikar people, who live in the Central Region of Cameroon, serve as a manifestation of their unique cultural identity. These items are proof of the Tikar's creative ability and rich cultural heritage because of their elaborate designs and symbolic significance.

One of the main features of Tikar handicraft are the finely crafted wooden masks. These masks, which are often decorated with intricate designs and vivid colors, are essential to many customs and celebrations. Since masks are said to help bridge the gap between the living and the afterlife, each one is a work of art that embodies both spiritual and aesthetic value.

Another distinctive feature of the Tikar people's creative legacy is their masterful beading. Beaded accessories like necklaces, bracelets, and ceremonial clothing exhibit an amazing level of intricacy. In addition to being aesthetically pleasing, Tikar beadwork's vivid hues and geometric designs have cultural significance that often allude to elements of the natural world, spirituality, and social standing in the community.

Tikar pottery is a unique creative expression that is separate from masks and beading. The distinctive forms and ornamental themes of the ceramics are indicative of the Tikar people's close relationship with the land. These artistically designed yet practical containers bring a little of tradition into everyday life, serving both ceremonial and utilitarian functions.

The artifacts of the Tikar people are more than just physical items; they are stores of cultural stories. Every artwork conveys a narrative, whether it is the account of a momentous event, a depiction of religious convictions, or an illustration of the Tikar people's bond with their surroundings. The Tikar people use the items as a visual language to convey and safeguard their cultural legacy for future generations.

You can get up close and personal with these fascinating items by visiting Tikar communities. Markets and craft fairs are transformed into lively venues where Tikar artists present their works, providing a window into the nexus between custom and modern art. The objects of the Tikar people entice admirers to discover the depth of Tikar workmanship and the rich tapestry of their cultural history because of their eternal beauty and cultural relevance.

Chapter 11

Savoring cuisine from Cameroon

Leading restaurants in Cameroon

With its many different areas, Cameroon's excellent restaurants provide a great gastronomic experience among its rich cultural variety. La Parisienne is a prominent restaurant in the busy city of Yaoundé, renowned for its exquisite French food and sophisticated atmosphere. Meanwhile, Muna Kalati, with its assortment of traditional foods, reflects the essence of Cameroonian tastes in Douala, the commercial center.

Stepping out into the bustling streets of Buea, The Junction is a local and tourist favorite, offering a blend of foreign and Cameroonian cuisines. Maquis du Nord, in Bamenda, farther north, draws customers with its homey ambiance and real Northwest fare.

When visiting the seaside town of Limbe, visitors may enjoy a meal that includes fresh seafood and regional dishes in a charming setting with a view of the Atlantic Ocean at Chariot Restaurant. Heading east to Garoua, Chez Moussa offers a distinctive dining experience while showcasing the northern region's culinary tradition.

La Palme d'Or, a gastronomic treasure in the sleepy village of Foumban, is renowned for its creative presentation of dishes that draw inspiration from the Western Highlands. Every area of Cameroon reveals a unique gastronomic tapestry as you travel through its varied landscapes; thus, dining at its best restaurants is like taking a trip through the core of the nation's cuisines.

Regional specialties

Cameroon's cuisine is a delightful fusion of many ethnic influences, and sampling the regional specialties is a great way to get a taste of the country's rich cultural heritage. It is impossible to talk about Cameroonian food without bringing up Ndolé, a filling delicacy that comes from the shore. This aromatic mixture of bitterleaf, peanuts, and various proteins like shrimp, pork, or fish creates a delicious, textured bite.

The famous meal of fufu and eru takes on a new role as we go inland. This traditional dinner consists of a starchy side dish called eru, which is often prepared from plantains or cassava, and a flavorful soup cooked with meat, vegetables, and a touch of spice. The social element of sharing a pot of fufu and eru gives the eating experience a new depth.

The well-known Pepper Soup provides a mouthwatering combination of spicy spices, herbs, and a variety of protein, such as goat meat or fish, for people who want their food hot and spicy. This meal is loved not only for its strong tastes but also for what the locals consider to be its therapeutic properties, which have the ability to revitalize.

The delicacy known as Achu and Yellow Soup, found in the western highlands, demonstrates the people's sophisticated cooking abilities. A lot of work goes into making this dish, such as mashing the cocoyams to make them smooth and pliable. A culinary masterwork, the accompanying yellow soup is crafted with a variety of ingredients that perfectly match the Achu.

A trip through Cameroonian cuisine wouldn't be complete without sampling the delicious street cuisine. "Suya," or grilled fish with plantains, is a common treat that can be found in busy marketplaces and on street corners. It provides a fast and filling sample of regional cuisine.

In the end, Cameroonian regional specialties are more than simply food; they capture the essence of the country and celebrate the variety of culinary customs that have been handed down through the ages, allowing both residents and tourists to indulge in a mouthwatering cultural mosaic.

The Experience of Street Food

Street cuisine in Cameroon is a bright tapestry that presents a thrilling sensory experience, with a wide variety of mouthwatering tastes and fragrances filling the busy streets and marketplaces. The aroma of spices and the sizzling sounds of grills entice you to go on a gastronomic journey that captures the essence of the nation as you stroll through the busy streets of Douala or Yaoundé.

In Cameroon, it is impossible to discuss street cuisine without bringing up the omnipresent Grilled Fish. The fragrance of freshly caught fish being skillfully grilled fills the air around anything from improvised kiosks to busy markets, drawing in both interested tourists and residents. A smokey depth is added to every exquisite mouthful by the precisely charred skin laced with a blend of spices, making the experience as much about the atmosphere as it is about the food.

Next to the fish grills, golden-fried plantains await your culinary delight. These starchy treats, whether grilled or fried, provide a savory and sweet counterpoint to the fish's smokey flavor. People from all walks of life love the traditional street food experience known as "Suya," which consists of grilled fish and plantains.

The vivid colors of the fruits and vegetables draw your attention as you make your way further into the maze-like marketplaces, indicating the arrival of another hidden gem of street cuisine: the brilliant and reviving Fruit Salad. These beautifully sliced and plated fruit salads are a lovely diversion from the busy world around them, bursting with freshness with every bite.

The fragrant appeal of Pepper Soup is too strong for those who like spicy food. This hot and spicy soup, which may be prepared with fish, beef, or a mix of the two, is a favorite among residents looking for a filling and tasty fix for street food.

In Cameroon, street food is more than simply delicious cuisine—it's a celebration of culture and community. People assemble around communal tables, laughing and telling tales over platters of delectable food, and conversations flow easily. With their varied menus, the street food stalls go beyond being simple merchants and take on the role of cultural ambassadors, enticing passersby to indulge in the vibrant and varied culinary mosaic that characterizes Cameroonian street food culture.

Dining Traditions

Dining in Cameroon is a very cultural experience that goes beyond simple nourishment, showcasing the many customs and beliefs that characterize this country in West Africa. The sharing of food is a very symbolic gesture that represents hospitality, solidarity, and the richness of community life.

Cameroonian eating habits are centered upon communal meals, frequently with friends and extended family. Social ties may be strengthened during get-togethers around a table, and there's a noticeable camaraderie to these dinners. The communal aspect of eating highlights the value of connections in Cameroonian society, regardless of whether one is dining in an urban center or a remote community.

Fufu and eru are two other examples of foods that represent the idea of dining together, since they are often consumed in groups. The center fufu pot and the bowl of eru that goes with it serve as gathering places for the community, promoting animated discussions and the sharing of tales. This kind of group meal promotes a feeling of unity and camaraderie.

In Cameroon, showing hospitality is highly valued, and visitors are often shown the highest regard and kindness. It is normal for hosts to go above and above to make sure their visitors are comfortable and nourished. This generosity strengthens the sense of community that pervades Cameroonian culture by extending beyond one's immediate family to encompass neighbors and even strangers.

Hand washing before meals is a cultural practice that emphasizes tidiness and consideration for the communal eating area.

Water basins are often seen before to eating spaces, highlighting how important hygiene is as a necessary component of the dining experience.

Moreover, there is careful protocol when it comes to exchanging meals. As a show of respect, elderly are often served first, and younger people in the group typically wait to start eating until the elders have finished. The deeply rooted principles of respect for hierarchy and age are reflected in this cultural subtlety.

The rich variety of Cameroonian cuisine is shown during lavish feasts that often accompany traditional festivities and festivals. These events emphasize the culinary prowess of regional communities and the diversity and depth of dishes that represent the nation's rich cultural diversity.

Essentially, Cameroonian dining customs are more than just an eating custom; they represent a celebration of the nation's complex tapestry of traditions, shared values, and community. The dinner table takes on symbolic significance as a place to foster connections, share tales, and maintain a sense of community throughout generations.

Chapter 12

Departure and Travel Tips

Souvenirs and Handicrafts

Cameroon has a wide selection of handicrafts and souvenirs that showcase the lively customs of the nation. The workmanship that captures the spirit of Cameroon's cultural legacy is so compelling that it is impossible to visit the marketplaces and artisanal centers without being enthralled by it.

Visitors are met with a stunning selection of handwoven textiles, vivid batik fabrics, and finely carved wooden sculptures in the busy marketplaces of Douala and Yaoundé. These mementos serve as physical representations of Cameroon's cultural identity, in addition to showcasing the creative talent of regional craftsmen. The vivid hues and designs seen in the textiles often narrate tales of custom and history, providing a unique window into the cultural histories of the several ethnic groups that inhabit Cameroon.

In Cameroon, woodcarving is a highly valued skill that yields beautiful masks, sculptures, and ceremonial items. The ancient patterns and significant motifs that have been handed down through the years are brought to life by the deft hands of craftspeople. Every item conveys a narrative, whether it is the commemoration of a noteworthy cultural occasion or the portrayal of ancestor spirits. The fine intricacies and cultural importance incorporated into these wooden works of art often captivate visitors.

There is a wide selection of beaded and brass accessories in Cameroon's marketplaces for individuals who like jewelry. The artisan's commitment to maintaining their cultural legacy is seen in the skill with which these ornaments were made. Every item, whether it be an earring, bracelet, or necklace, captures the unique styles of Cameroon's many ethnic groups.

Beyond the material, Cameroonian souvenirs have an enduring charm. It's an opportunity to engage with the legends and customs that have molded the nation's populace and to dig into the center of the cultural tapestry of the nation. A trip through Cameroon's souvenirs is an exploration of the spirit of a country, whether one chooses to immerse oneself in the craft villages scattered throughout the countryside or peruse the artisan booths in the busy metropolis.

Essentially, souvenirs and handicrafts from Cameroon are more than just trinkets; they are cultural ambassadors that invite visitors to bring a little bit of the country's rich history home with them. Every well-produced object reminds us of the rich and varied tapestry that makes up this country in West Africa.

Tips for Health and Safety

Like any foreign trip, traveling to Cameroon necessitates taking precautions for your health and safety in order to have a safe and happy trip. Here are some crucial pointers for keeping yourself well when visiting this vibrantly culturally diverse country in Africa, including anything from tropical illnesses to distinctive regional traditions.

1. Health Precautions: Make sure you have the required immunizations and prescriptions by speaking with your doctor well in advance of your trip. Typhoid, malaria prophylaxis, and yellow fever vaccinations are common vaccinations.
Keep a basic first-aid kit with you that includes bandages, antiseptic wipes, painkillers, and any prescription drugs you may have on hand.

2. Food and Water Safety: Savor the exciting food scene, but proceed with care while consuming street food. To reduce your chance of contracting a foodborne disease, choose well-cooked meals and stay away from raw or undercooked foods.
To avoid contracting waterborne illnesses, use bottled or filtered water. Steer clear of using ice in your beverages unless you are certain that it is sourced safely.

3. Insect Protection: Wear long sleeves and trousers and apply insect repellent with DEET, particularly at dusk and morning when mosquitoes are most active, considering the prevalence of malaria in certain areas.

If you are staying in a more rural region where there may be a greater risk of malaria transmission, make sure you sleep beneath a mosquito net.

4. Sun Safety: The tropical environment of Cameroon implies exposure to intense sunlight. To avoid becoming sick from the sun, wear a hat, drink plenty of water, and apply sunscreen often.

5. Local Customs and Etiquette: Learn about the customs of the area to be respectful and prevent inadvertent offense. For instance, shaking hands is a popular way to welcome someone, and using your right hand for gestures and conversations is the norm.

Acquire some basic French and local language skills to improve your ability to communicate and create a good rapport with the people you meet.

6. Transportation Safety: When using public transportation, abide by the safety instructions. Use reliable transportation options, keep your car in good working order, and buckle up when you can.
Keep an eye on the state of the roads, particularly in rural regions, and modify your itinerary as necessary.

7. Emergency Readiness: Keep emergency numbers on your phone and be aware of the closest hospitals' locations. Think about getting emergency medical coverage and, if necessary, evacuation coverage when buying travel insurance.

8. Remain Updated: Pay attention to travel warnings and remain up-to-date on local affairs. In case of an emergency, familiarize yourself with the addresses of the embassies and consulates of your nation.

To put it simply, a knowledgeable and well-prepared tourist is better able to handle the particular difficulties of visiting Cameroon. You can truly appreciate the natural beauty and cultural diversity that this West African country has to offer by putting your health and safety first. Happy travels!

Concluding Words on Touring Cameroon

Here are a few last tips to make the most of your time in Cameroon and optimize your experience while you explore this fascinating West African country. Here's how to end your journey on a good note, including everything from cultural experiences to breathtaking natural formations.

1. Welcome Cultural Variety: There are many different ethnic groups in Cameroon, each with their own customs, dialects, and ceremonies. Spend time getting to know the people, going to cultural gatherings, and being fully immersed in Cameroon's rich legacy.

2. Explore the Markets: Stroll around the humming marketplaces in Yaoundé and Douala. These lively centers provide a kaleidoscope of hues, scents, and noises, offering a unique chance to buy mementos,

engage with craftspeople, and savor regional specialties.

3. Explore the Natural World: Cameroon is a naturalist's paradise. Discover the breathtaking Mount Cameroon, meander through the thick jungles, and explore the verdant Western Highlands. The natural beauties of Cameroon will not disappoint you, whether you like trekking, birding, or seeing animals.

4. Savor Local Cuisine: Savor the variety of tastes found in Cameroonian food. The diverse cuisine of the nation is reflected in the meals, which range from fragrant soups to fiery grilled seafood. For a memorable gastronomic experience, don't miss out on delicacies like Ndolé, Eru, and common street food.

5. Attend Festivals and Events: Look up any regional celebrations and events that could take place while you're in town on the calendar. These festivities provide an up-close look at Cameroon's colorful customs, complete with dancing, music, and social events that highlight the country's character.

6. Connect with Wildlife: To see Cameroon's amazing biodiversity, visit wildlife reserves like Waza National Park or Limbe Wildlife Centre. The nation's dedication to conservation offers the opportunity to see and assist efforts to maintain its distinctive wildlife, which includes magnificent elephants and uncommon primates.

7. Opportunities for Photography: Through your lens, capture the soul of Cameroon. The nation is full of photographic opportunities, from vibrant marketplaces to breathtaking scenery. When taking pictures of individuals, remember to ask permission and show respect for local traditions.

8. "Think and Unwind Spend a minute thinking back on your adventure. Discover a peaceful location to take in the sights and sounds, such as the placid ambiance by the lakes or the soft waves along the Atlantic coast. Give yourself some time to unwind and take in the beauty all around you.

9. Keep an open mind and welcome the unexpected. Cameroon's spontaneity is often

what makes it so charming. Be willing to try new things, interact with a variety of people, and let the pulse of the nation direct your travels.

In the big climax of your journey, Cameroon shows itself to be a place that goes beyond simple travel and instead transforms into a tapestry of relationships, memories, and experiences. Take with you the warmth of its people and the impression of its varied landscapes engraved in your heart as you say adieu to this amazing country. I hope your vacation memories of Cameroon last as long as its rich cultural history. Safe travels.

Printed in Great Britain
by Amazon